# A Peek into Aunt Helen's Closet
## An Introduction to a World Traveler

Ellen Mnich & Anita DeSarbo

*R.J.*
*We all smile in the same language.*

*Ellen Mnich*
*AKA Aunt Helen*

Special Thanks
Bill Mnich, Bob DeSarbo,
Robyn Mangini, and Dina Fisher

Cover and book design by The Troy Book Makers

Printed in the United States of America

The Troy Book Makers • Troy, New York
www.thetroybookmakers.com

Aunt Helen's Closet: A Museum Approach to Education is a registered trademark.

To find out more or book an event visit www.aunthelenscloset.com
To order additional copies of this title visit www.tbmbooks.com

ISBN: 978-1-61468-007-9

*1909-1996*

"We are more alike than unalike, my friends, in minor ways we differ, in major we're the same. We all teach each other, we all learn from each other, we all love with the same heart."

—Maya Angelou

Helen Fitzgerald was a tiny woman with bright red hair who fulfilled a lifelong dream to travel the world. Forging forward in a time when women did not travel alone to remote parts of the world, she traveled and collected ordinary things, filling bags of all shapes and sizes.

Eventually her old and ordinary house in an ordinary small town in Cohoes, New York overflowed with the objects that now tell the story of the ordinary people that she met as she traveled the world.

Although Helen was a woman of few words due to a speech disability which sometimes made it difficult for others to understand her, the collection speaks for her and for all the people of the world promoting understanding of both the sameness and differences inherent in all of us.

In Aunt Helen's world, we all smile in the same language.

Welcome to
Aunt Helen's Closet

Home is where the story begins.

Time after time, exhausted but excited to plan her next adventure, Aunt Helen, citizen of the world, arrived back at her old stone house. Sashaying across her Persian rug in her favorite slippers with the turned up toes, she was quickly surrounded by the magic of her exotic treasures and ever-present memories.

To travel the world in her footsteps, just step inside Aunt Helen's Closet.

Living a never ending life of comings and goings, Aunt Helen often paused to admire the vast collection of exotic treasures that overflowed from her cluttered closet and remained scattered throughout every room in her comfortable old house.

The parlor walls were dripping with unusual collections; gigantic colorful fans from China, carved wooden masks from Africa, and shells collected from far-away beaches. Shelves came alive with dolls, puppets and animals perched side-by-side eager to tell their tales of distant lands.

And in the corner, door ajar, loomed the mammoth closet bursting with huge bins, bags and boxes of souvenirs beckoning a visitor to the far ends of the earth.

Clothes tumbled half on and half off hangers, baskets overflowed with rich silks from Thailand, hand embroidered leathers from Egypt and plush velvets from France.

A fancy red and gold kimono from Japan, a huge multicolored sombrero from Mexico and an armadillo pocketbook adorned the closet door.

Like the treasures in her closet, Aunt Helen was extraordinary and unique.

Aunt Helen wore a colorful caftan in Mexico, a batik djebela in Africa and a goatskin coat in Afghanistan.

Aunt Helen was a dreamer. As a child, devouring
books and cutting out pictures of distant places, she
dreamed of traveling around the world. Armchair tours
of the wonders of the world led to planning, packing
and finally 60 years of traveling and collecting.

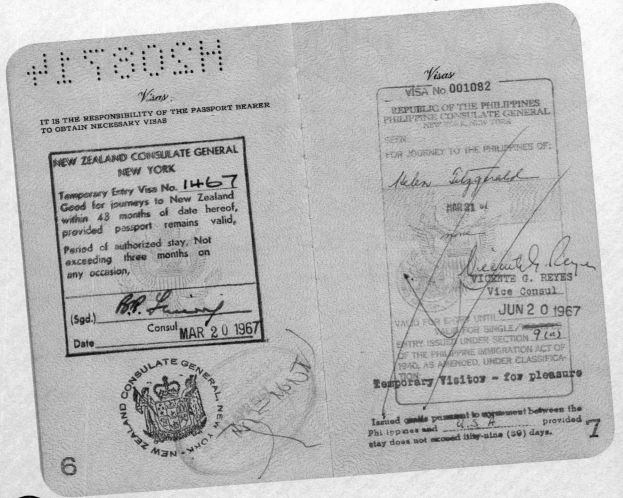

I think I hear Honolulu calling my name. I can almost feel the sands of the Sahara desert in my shoes.

As a young woman in 1930 with her itinerary in hand, Aunt Helen embarked on her first journey. But it wasn't a boat ride on the Hudson River that flowed near her house in upstate New York. Instead she floated and fished for giant catfish on the Amazon River in South America.

This was the first of many exciting journeys and the beginning of the amazing collection.

*A wall hanging from Peru reminded Aunt Helen of her many fishing expeditions.*

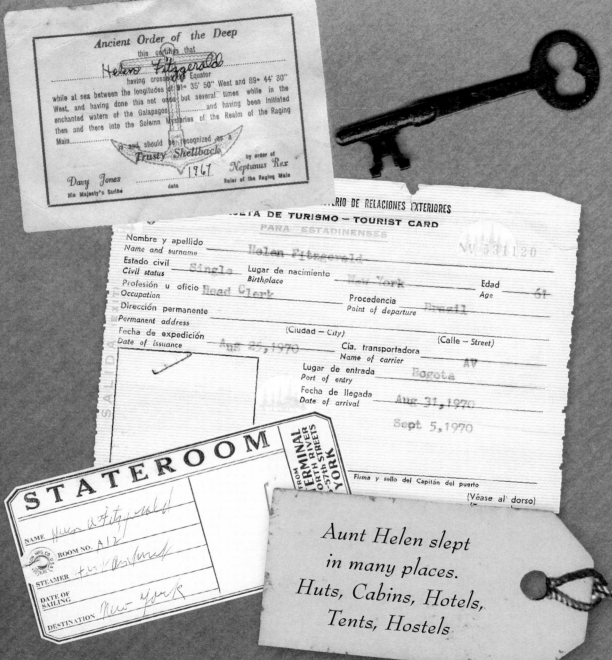

**Ancient Order of the Deep**

this certifies that

*Helen Fitzgerald*

having crossed the Equator
while at sea between the longitudes of 91° 35' 50" West and 89° 44' 30"
West, and having done this not once but several times while in the
enchanted waters of the Galapagos .............. and having been initiated
then and there into the Solemn Mysteries of the Realm of the Raging
Main.............. is and should be recognized as a

*Trusty Shellback*                        by order of

1967

**Davy Jones** .............. **Neptunus Rex**
His Majesty's Scribe          date          Ruler of the Raging Main

---

......RIO DE RELACIONES EXTERIORES

......TA DE TURISMO — TOURIST CARD

PARA ESTADINENSES                    N° 531120

Nombre y apellido
*Name and surname* —— Helen Fitzgerald

Estado civil        Single      Lugar de nacimiento                        Edad
*Civil status*                   *Birthplace*        New York             *Age*    61

Profesión u oficio  Head Clerk
*Occupation*                              Procedencia
                                          *Point of departure*   Brazil

Dirección permanente
*Permanent address*
                              (Ciudad — City)                    (Calle — Street)

Fecha de expedición                      Cía. transportadora
*Date of issuance*   Aug 25, 1970        *Name of carrier*             AV

                                          Lugar de entrada
                                          *Port of entry*       Bogota

                                          Fecha de llegada
                                          *Date of arrival*     Aug 31, 1970

                                          Sept 5, 1970

                              Firma y sello del Capitán del puerto

                                                      (Véase al dorso)

---

**STATEROOM**

TERMINAL
NORTH RIVER
W. 57th STREETS
....YORK

NAME  Helen A Fitzgerald

ROOM NO.  A 12

STEAMER

DATE OF
SAILING

DESTINATION  New York

---

*Aunt Helen slept
in many places.
Huts, Cabins, Hotels,
Tents, Hostels*

13

[P. & I.—44.]

## PASSENGER LANDING PERMIT.

Immigration Restriction Ordinance, Ch. 20. No. 2, Section 13.

NAME OF SHIP......**S.S. FORT AMHERST**..........

PASSENGER NAME ....Helen Fitzgerald..........

AS SUPPLIED TO THE IMMIGRATION DEPARTMENT ON PASSENGER'S MANIFEST.

Permission to land in the Colony during the Ship's stay in Port is hereby granted to the Passenger referred to above.

Yuille—y 2153

## PASSENGER LIST

### OAKLAND — YOKOHAMA
Rev. and Mrs. Harry A. Engeman . . . Chicago, Illinois

### OAKLAND — CRUISE — LOS ANGELES
Miss Elizabeth H. Andersen . . . . . . . . . . . . . . . . . .
Miss Nina E. Andersen . . . . . . . . Southbury, Connecticut
Mrs. Harold J. Elmendorf . . . . . . . Southbury, Connecticut
Miss Helen Fitzgerald . . . . . . . . . Southbury, Connecticut
Mr. Spencer Mann . . . . . . . . . . . Cohoes, New York
Mrs. Louise M. McCarroll . . . . . . . Isle of Palms, South Carolina
Miss Grace Tessier . . . . . . . . . . Southbury, Connecticut
. . . . . . . . Southbury, Connecticut

### OAKLAND — CRUISE — OAKLAND
Mr. Gil and Mrs. Grace Anderson . . . Hayward, California
Mrs. William W. Wood . . . . . . . . Seattle, Washington

By order of his Oceanic Majesty,

3⁴⁸ **Neptunus Rex**

*it is hereby certified that*

**Helen A. Fitzgerald**

having, in the presence of His Majesty's
good and faithful servants of

**MOORE-McCORMACK LINES**

met the tests prescribed for all who approach His Equatorial Court
is forthwith proclaimed a WORTHY SHELLBACK

ATTEST _____ **JESSE R. HODGES** _____ CAPTAIN, S. S. _____ "BRAZIL"

(Custodian of Royal Fin)

Date _____ **JULY 15th, 1955**

---

**AMERICAN PRESIDENT LINES**

**S.S. PRESIDENT TRUMAN**

Voyage No. 73

*...iling from Oakland on January 25th, 1979*

In Orient Service

*...ommanding*

---

*Captain*

L.S. GOLTZER

*Cordially Invites*

Miss Helen Fitzgerald

*to a*

*Cocktail Party Aboard*

*S S* PRESIDENT...

*Place*

PASSENGER LOUNGE

*Dat...*

26 Janu...

*King Neptune gives his
permission for Aunt Helen
to cross the equator.*

From that day on, nothing stopped Aunt Helen. From Argentina to Tanzania, she wandered and collected. She rode on every beast of burden known to mankind; a camel in Egypt, an elephant in Thailand, and a donkey in the Grand Canyon. She walked beside a llama in the Andes Mountains and was even seen chased by a sea lion in the Galapagos Islands.

The tiny porcelain replicas of the animals Aunt Helen encountered all over the world continued to tell her stories from the closet shelves.

*Aunt Helen kept in touch with friends by sending letters and postcards.*

Aunt Helen, clomping along on a dirt road with a turbaned driver.

Aunt Helen was an ordinary woman living an
extraordinary life. She was eccentric and outrageous,
a skinny woman with blazing red hair that stuck out
this way and that. She was also daring, brave, kind and
curious about all places and customs of the world.

Loving life and people of all shapes, sizes and colors,
Aunt Helen longed to experience everyone and everything.

*Aunt Helen collected stamps,
one of her many hobbies.*

Never one to miss a celebration, Aunt Helen taught us to savor every moment. She wished her friends good health and prosperity in 17 different languages.

| | |
|---|---|
| Bohemian: Naz Dar | (Naz-Dar') |
| Brazilian: Sau'de | (Sah-oo'day) |
| Dutch: Proost | (Prohst) |
| Finnish: Kippis | (Kee'pees) |
| French: Sante' | (Sahn'tay) |
| German: Prosit | (Proh'zit) |
| Greek: Eis Igian | (Ees igee'an) |
| Hebrew: Lehayim | Leh-hah'yim) |
| Irish: Sl'ainte | (Slahn'cha) |
| Itailan: Salute | (Sa-loo'tay) |
| Japanese: Kampai | (Kahm-pah'ee) |
| Norwegian: Skal | (Skohl) |
| Polish: Na Zdrowie | (Na Zdruh'vyeh) |
| Scotch: Shlante | (Shlahn"tay) |
| Spanish: Salud | (Sa-lood') |
| Turkish; Serese | (Sheh-reh'say) |
| Welsh: Iechyd Da | (Yeh'hid Dah) |

Wherever Aunt Helen was at the moment was her favorite place and whatever she was wearing was her favorite outfit. If she noticed someone was poor or hungry, she would ask to buy what they were wearing or making. She would examine it, ask how it was made, buy it and bring it home.

But Aunt Helen wouldn't just put an outfit away in her closet full of memories; she would use it, wear it and show it off.

*Aunt Helen loved her horsehide coat from Argentina.*

Only Aunt Helen
would tour Greece
in an outrageously
mismatched outfit:
a skirt from Spain, a
blouse from Turkey,
and a pocketbook from
Egypt to finish it off.

Mohammaden Mosque
Trinidad, Spain

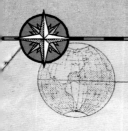

# Copeland Travel Agency

XXXXXXXX STREET     TROY     AS. 2-7342
2 - 4 Second     NEW YORK

_At 1st flight 610_

## ROUND THE WORLD FLIGHT SCHEDULE FOR MISS HELEN FITZGERALD

All flights confirmed to arrival BOMBAY

| | | | | | | 328 | | 3:00PM | | 3:53PM |
|---|---|---|---|---|---|---|---|---|---|---|
| Thu Jul 26 | – | ALBANY | – | IDLEWILD | F MO ~~24~~ | | departs ~~7:15AM~~ | arrives | | ~~8:08AM~~ |
| " " " | – | IDLEWILD | – | ATHENS | YJTW 800 | " | 7:30PM | " | | 2:55PM7/ |
| Sun Jul 29 | – | ATHENS | – | ISTANBUL | T BE 256 | " | 6:55PM | " | 8:05PM | |
| The Jul 31 | – | ISTAHBUL | – | BEIRUT | T LH 606 | " | 9:35PM | " | 10:55PM | |
| ~~Wed~~ Aug 1 | – | BEIRUT | – | JERUSALEM | T LN 187 | " | 8:15AM | " | 19:15AM | |
| Sat Aug 4 | – | JERUSALEM | – | CAIRO | T JN 501 | " | 10:45AM | " | 1:55PM | |
| Wed Aug 8 | – | CAIRO | – | NAIROBI | T AF 465 | " | 5:20AM | " | 10:55AM | |
| Sat Aug 11 | – | NAIROBI | – | ENTEBBE | T EC 015 | " | 7:30AM | " | 10:35AM | |
| Mon Aug 13 | – | ENTEBBE | – | NAIROBI | T EC 018 | " | 4:00PM | " | 6:05PM | |

(No stop-over permitted on second call at Nairobi - the above connection
is legal; it is the closest one we could get)

| | | | | | | | | |
|---|---|---|---|---|---|---|---|---|
| Tue Aug 14 | – | NAIROBI | – | BOMBAY | T EC 736 | " | 12:15AM | " 12:45PM T |

Flights from here on are suggested; no reservations have been made after
Bombay

| BOMBAY | – | DELHI | daily (3) . | IC 181 d. 7:30AM - Ar. 10:30AM, also 11:00AM and 6:00PM |
|---|---|---|---|---|
| DELHI | – | SRINIGAR | daily (2) | IC 425 d. 8:00AM - Ar. 10:00AM, also 11 |
| SRINIGAR | | | | 6 d. 10:45AM - Ar. 12:45PM with DELHI, second trip allowed |
| DELHI | | | | 0 d. 4:00PM - Ar. 6:50PM |
| BEIRUT | | | | 0 d. 7:30PM - Ar. 9:35PM |
| Aug | | | | 4 d. 7:40AM - Ar. 2:05PM |
| Aug | | | | 5 d. 2:15PM - Ar. 7:45PM, also 12:5 |
| Aug | | | | d. 2:50PM - Ar. 4:50PM |
| | – | DJAKARTA | daily, all | GA 552 d. 6:40AM - Ar. 7:50AM |

_The tour begins
in Athens, Greece
July 26, 1962_

# Copeland Travel Agency

28 STATE STREET
~~XXXXXXXX~~
2 – 4 Second

TROY
NEW YORK

AS. 2-7342

Miss Fitzgerald

SURABAYA –
Sun Sep  2 – BANDJARMASIN – (only)      GA 572 d. 9:20AM ar. 11:00AM
~~BALIKPAPAN~~(Sun)

Tue Sep  4 – BANDJARMASIN – once a      GA 524 d. 1:20PM ar.  2:55PM
BALIKPAPAN   week

Wed Sep  5 – BALIKPAPAN –   once a      GA 525 d. 7:00AM ar.  8:35AM
BANDJARMASIN   week

~~Service from Djakarta, via Surabaya~~ to Bandjarmasin, and vice-versa, is
frequent.  The flight from Bandjarmasin to Balikpapan is once a week only, as
above.

Wed Sep  5 – BANDJARMASIN – daily       GA 593 d. 11:50AM ar. 4:10PM
DJAKARTA
On return to DJAKARTA, no stop-over permitted, the above connection is OK

Thu Sep  6 – DJAKARTA –    once a       GA 900 d.  6:30AM ar. 12:05PM
MANILA    week

Sat Sep  8 – MANILA-HONG KONG daily,    CX 326 d.  7:30PM ar. 10:45PM
different times

Service from here is daily, although different times, and different airlines:

Tue Sep 11 – HONG Kong-TOKYO            PA   2 d.  6:30PM ar. 10:15PM

Mon Sep 17 – TOKYO-HONOLULU             JA 800    9:00AM "   9:25PM (9/16)

Tue Sep 18 – HONOLULU –LOS ANGELES      JA 860   12:20PM "   8:30PM

Wed Sep 19 – LOS ANGELES-MEXICO CI                          5:25PM

Thu Sep 27 – MEXICO CITY-IDLEWILD

Thu Sep 27 – IDLEWILD – ALBNY

*Home bound from*
*Mexico City, Mexico*
*September 28, 1963*

BY _____
COPELAND TRAVEL AGENCY
July 23, 1962

In Costa Rica, Aunt Helen wore a fabulous green outfit adorned with tiny mirrors that reflected the sunlight when she walked. At home, it hung in her closet next to a jeweled belt from the Thailand, alongside the shiny black clockabook from Las Vegas and the nine foot silk sari from India.

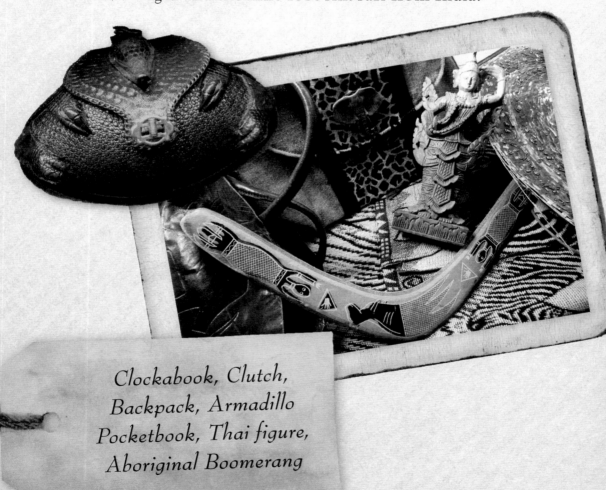

*Clockabook, Clutch, Backpack, Armadillo Pocketbook, Thai figure, Aboriginal Boomerang*

Aunt Helen began each trip with her favorite armadillo pocketbook on her arm and returned with at least one other interesting bag full of trinkets from every place she visited.

When her bag was full, Aunt Helen bought another. In Argentina, she bought a knitted bag with wooden handles. She carried a bag of woven grass in the Bahamas. In France, Aunt Helen bartered for a beautiful tapestry bag. Most unusual was the camel skin bag she carried in Morocco. It was tanned with camel urine.

When she was not able to cram one more souvenier into the overflowing closet, Aunt Helen proudly displayed her favorites on the bedroom wall.

*There are many time zones around the world. I wonder if Aunt Helen ever missed a plane.*

Outside the huge closet were hats, scarves and jewelry swaying on a revolving rack that sometimes moved and sometimes didn't. Aunt Helen never worried about her clothes and accessories matching. Planning another trip was always on her mind.

*Every Traveler Needs a Hat. Cowboy Hat, Beret, Baseball Cap, Sombrero, Straw Hat, Babushka, Mantilla*

# Aunt Helen

**OUTRAGEOUS**

Eccentric

**Adventurous**

UNUSUAL

**Kind**

*Loving*

𝔊enerous

Intriguing

*Aunt Helen traveled for over 60 years from 1930 to the 1990s.*

Aunt Helen purchased or bartered for clothes, hats, shoes and jewelry all over the world. Then she wore her extraordinary clothes everywhere, to the store, to church, to work, on her trips. and even sitting on her front porch. Her friends liked to guess where she had recently traveled whenever a new outfit appeared.

Captain Jesse R. Hodges
*Cordially invites you to attend a*

Reception

In Honor Of

His Eminence

Francis Cardinal Spellman

**Saturday, August 6th, 1955**
*at six-thirty o'clock in the evening*

At Sea                                                    S. S. Brazil

*Born in 1909, Aunt Helen lived in every decade of the 20th century.*

Aunt Helen was proud to announce that she visited every country in the world, except two, England and one she couldn't remember. She also traveled to every state in the United States and of course, she liked her own home best.

## Exploring the 50 states of the United States of America

| | | | |
|---|---|---|---|
| Alabama | Indiana | Nebraska | South Carolina |
| Alaska | Iowa | Nevada | South Dakota |
| Arizona | Kansas | New Hampshire | Tennessee |
| Arkansas | Kentucky | New Jersey | Texas |
| California | Louisiana | New Mexico | Utah |
| Colorado | Maine | New York | Vermont |
| Connecticut | Maryland | North Carolina | Virginia |
| Delaware | Massachusetts | North Dakota | Washington |
| Florida | Michigan | Ohio | West Virginia |
| Georgia | Minnesota | Oklahoma | Wisconsin |
| Hawaii | Mississippi | Oregon | Wyoming |
| Idaho | Missouri | Pennsylvania | |
| Illinois | Montana | Rhode Island | |

The longest continuous friendly border in the world is between the United States and its northern neighbor, Canada.

ROYAL HAWAIIAN HOTEL
HONOLULU, T. H.

FITZGERALD MISS HELEN

$51
646    6-1-53    1L
PERSONAL    ACC    MON

B    426

| MEMO. | DATE | EXPLANATION | CHARGES | CREDITS | BAL. DUE |
|---|---|---|---|---|---|
| | | | ★ 0.15 | | ★ 0.15 |
| 1 | JUN-1-5 | ONE | ★ 0.77 | | ★ 0.92 |
| | | AR    SURF | ★ 1.73 | | ★ 2.65 |
| | | PdOut | ★ 1.50 | | 4.15 |
| | | PdOut | | | |

*Hawaiian Airlines*

E Na Hoaloha
TO ALL FRIENDS

Leinaala
(fragrant garland of flowers)    THE BEARER

OF THIS PALAPALA (CERTIFICATE) WAS A PASSENGER ABOARD THE SS LURLINE DURING ITS VOYAGE

FROM    Honolulu    TO    Los Angeles

During this time she did complete lessons in the
art of doing the Polynesian Dance called the HULA.
Let it therefore be known that this certificate permits
the bearer to perform the dance she has learned with
the best wishes of the Hula Goddess "LAKA."

S.S. LURLINE

LONGITUDE
LATITUDE

ISSUED THIS    DAY OF    195

*Little Brown Gal*

KA KUMU HULA O KA PAKIPIKA
(THE HULA TEACHER OF THE PACIFIC)

*Here's the proof.
Aunt Helen learned
to do the hula!*

LAST BALANCE IS AMOUNT DUE
UNLESS OTHERWISE INDICATED
BILLS ARE PAYABLE WHEN PRESENTED
RETAIN THIS RECEIPT

pleasant
have the pleasure of serving

After I left Wassaic I had a pleasant little ...
in Connecticut ... at the Sachh...
...ning School ... heen ...

Stockholm, N...

TOOMEY'S PAVILION
5Mi. NORTH OF GLENS FALLS
OFF 9L OR BAY ROAD

STOCKHOLM
21 3
66
A
35 SVERIGE

...len Fitzgerald
...nut St.
... N.Y.
...A.

MIAMI BEACH
JAN 25
FLA.

Boy this is
the place for a
vacation. Having a
wonderful time
see you soon
Mac N

2 U.S. POSTAGE

...swimming. See
ya soon.
Mary, Chuck, Peg & Terry
buildings at ...

Miss Helen Fitzgerald
Colwes, N.Y.

...ais. Last
... some friends
... me; it
... as Wassaic
... native ...

Aunt Helen hiked all over the world. She even made it to the top of Mt. Fiji in Japan. She hiked;

The Laurentian Mountains of Canada

The Green Mountains of Vermont

The White Mountains of New Hampshire

The Smokies and Rockies

The Foothills of Mt. Aconcagua in South America

Mt. Kilimanjaro in Africa

The Himalayas

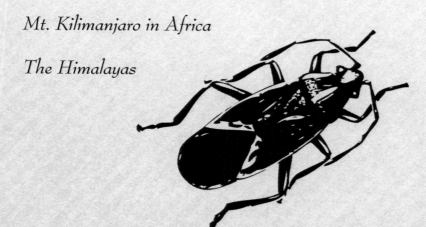

Aunt Helen wasn't a mountain climber.

She wasn't a rock climber.

She loved the outdoors.

She hiked in the foothills of the Himalyas because she wanted to see how other people lived.

Bugs-just part of the fun when you're in search of adventure.

Between trips Aunt Helen lived in a house not
unlike most of the houses on the narrow street in the
quaint waterfront community of Cohoes, New York.

Eager to set sail on her first adventure around
the world, Aunt Helen sold the house in 1943
to finance the trip. Much to her delight she was
able to buy the same house back 50 years later
in the same condition that she sold it in.

THIS IS TO CERTIFY that the following person
Helen Fitzgerald
is a resident of the City of Cohoes, County of Albany, and
State of New York, and is a qualified voter of the 5th Ward
5th Dist, and desires to visit British W. Indies,
for Virgin Islov, F W. Indies for 23 days
Countersigned: Rudolph Rowlier
Mayor, City of Cohoes.

Date June 14 1951

REPUBLIC OF CHINA
入境簽
13 FEB 1979
278

中華民國駐紐約總領事館
CONSULATE-GENERAL
OF THE REPUBLIC OF CHINA
NEW YORK
觀光簽證 (A)
TOURIST VISA
d until DEC 1 1982
for multiple journey(s)
e Republic of China if
rt remains valid.
Sun Yi Huey
SUN YI HUEY
CHANCELLOR of
RAL of
1978
Date of issue: DEC 1978
Duration of stay: ONE month
No. 714812 Fee: GRATIS

The porch needed painting and the shutters looked like crooked eyebrows framing an old wrinkled face. Stone turrets invited friends in to explore. Years later the outside was still old and uninteresting, yet inside every nook and cranny overflowed with boxes, bags and piles of exotic treasures.

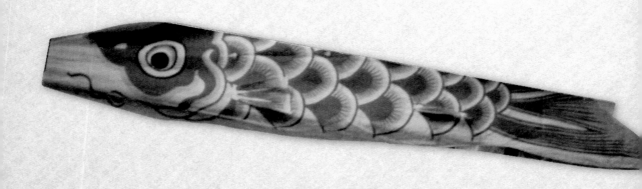

*Like the treasures she packed away in her old steamer trunk, Aunt Helen was extraordinary in every way.*

Like the collection that overwhelmed it, the house itself had an interesting story to tell. It was bursting with memories and the caretaker was Aunt Helen.

*Aunt Helen didn't say much. Her treasures said it all.*

Some days as she peered into the huge closet, Aunt Helen smiled and relived each and every wonderful escapade; rafting down the Zambezi River in Africa, going on a walk-about in Australia, and a safari in New Zealand.

She remembered cruising, camping, hiking, and paddling her way across continents as well as swimming, sailing and snorkeling from the African savannah to the Australian outback.

In her mind's eye she thought fondly of the snake charmers of Bangladesh and the entertaining street performers in Rio de Janiero.

Aunt Helen and a few friends are seen rafting on the Zambezi River in Africa.

Aunt Helen journeyed again and again to uncover the beauty, bounty and majesty of the earth's most sacred places.

The golden elephants on the outside of the bulging
brown leather satchel that Aunt Helen frequently dragged
into the house caught her eye. It reminded her of a visit
to the night market in Thailand where the mahouts
marched their elephants about. Beginning
each vacation empty, this
purse became Aunt
Helen's constant
companion.

*The houda sits on the*
*elephant's back. The*
*mahout is in charge of*
*commanding the elephant.*

Things to learn from Aunt Helen

*We all smile in the same language*
*Enjoy the moment*
*Have the courage to challenge yourself*
*Believe in yourself*
*See the world through Aunt Helen's eyes*

*Aunt Helen displayed her Southeast Asian artifact, a story burned into pieces of bamboo connected with string.*

Aunt Helen met different people, wore different clothes, ate different food, collected souvenirs and learned from the people she met all over the globe.

Anything Aunt Helen needed or wanted, she bought on her trips. When she was in Egypt, she wanted to look the way they did in Egypt. And when she was in Timbuktu, Kalamazoo and Ouagadougou, she wanted to look the way they did there too.

*Aunt Helen Enjoyed*
*Watching People*
*Artists, Potters, Weavers,*
*Lace Makers, Kite Makers,*
*Jewelry Makers*

FORM T-1003 (4-47)

# UNITED STATES CUSTOMS

Transportation Entry No. ____ I.T. 151570

From ____ NEW YORK ____ to ____

This package is under bond and must be delivered intact
to the chief officer of the customs at

____ ALBANY, NEW YORK ____

# WARNING

Two years' impris... or $5000 fine, or both, is the
... noval of this package or any of

PRINTED IN U.S.A.

---

11 necklaces | 2.50
earring | .50
Jug | 3.50
3 Vases | 1.50
2 Hats | 1.95
Ash tray | .50
7 pocket forks | 7.50
2 Kalitash | .70
5 Basket | 5.00
2 bracelet | 1.00
Chain | .75
2 Dolls | 11.50
Sandal | 5.00
 | 1.00

---

2 Fans | .75
2 Belt | 1.00
6 pins | 4.50
Clay Jug | .25
Picture | .70
Religious picture | 1.00
1 Kerchief | .80
1 Fan | .75
4 Canadian Club | 8.00
1 Scotch | 3.50

Aunt Helen wore a bright red shawl to cover her arms in Afghanistan, a crystal covered pink vest in Italy, a hand woven tunic in Switzerland and a fringed poncho in Chile. She wrapped herself in a sarong in Burma, and a golden silk bathrobe with loops instead of button holes in Japan.

Always on the search for unique accessories, necklaces of seeds, feathers, animal bones, terra-cota beads and sparkling jewels hung around her neck. One of a kind Thai ear cuffs sometimes adorned her unpierced ears or she might have been seen wearing her favorite banana bunch earrings.

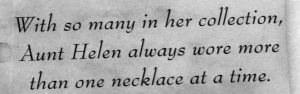

*With so many in her collection, Aunt Helen always wore more than one necklace at a time.*

A necklace from Nepal carved from animal bone tells a story too.

Returning home again and again, Aunt Helen emptied
the unusual objects from her near bursting bags, often
causing an avalanche of the treasures in the gigantic
closet. Hooks bent with the weight of a goatskin coat from
Afghanistan, a warm red wool cape from China, a hand
woven straw hat from Italy and her favorite snake skin belt.

Many times it seemed that not one more thing
could be squeezed into the huge closet,
but with each trip the collection
continued to grow.

*Colorful nesting dolls
from Poland looked down
from Aunt Helen's stone
fireplace mantle.*

Aunt Helen often laughed. "A bigger closet is what I need."

So Aunt Helen began to surround herself with the exotic treasures she collected. Irish lace curtains hung on her bedroom windows. A coo-coo clock from Germany announced every hour and a call to explore the evidence of Aunt Helen's escapades. Comfy chairs placed hither and yon throughout the cluttered parlor contributed to an invitation for a lingering stay.

Beautiful fans from several Asian countries were like wallpaper that helped to camouflage the peeling plaster of the old parlor walls.

Many years ago the airlines
gave each passenger
an interesting fan.
Aunt Helen added them
all to her collection.

Aunt Helen's table was set with dishes from China and crystal goblets from the Island of Murano were placed lovingly on a hand tatted lace tablecloth from Belgium. The sun shone through a one of a kind intricately carved teak room divider from Bali.

**WORLD WANDERER:** In her global travels, Helen Fitzgerald Cohoes has ridden an elephant in Nepal and been chased by lions on the Galapagos Islands. She has trekked to more 50 countries. (Photo by Luannne Ferris)

*Used by permission of the Times Union Albany, New York*

*Aunt Helen*
*Unique, Imaginative, Eccentric, Adventurous, Generous, Speech Impaired, Fascinating, Inspiring*

Guests were served Turkish coffee from a hand crafted ornate copper pot and offered snacks from one of the unusual sea shells that hung from a net in her living room.

Aunt Helen served coffee from the ornate copper coffee pot from Turkey.

A little lady with a ferocious appetite, Aunt Helen never missed an opportunity to sample the native cuisine. She tried sushi in Tokyo, calamari in Rome, croissants in Paris, and sauerkraut in Berlin. Although she loved to experiment with recipes she collected on her many trips, guests soon realized that Aunt Helen did not possess the best culinary skills.

*A Thai woman cooks in Thailand, the Land of Smiles.*

# FORTUNE COOKIES

*You are destined to be a world traveler!*

*You will learn to eat with chopsticks or maybe not!*

*You will meet many interesting people!*

## Ingredients
1 cup soft butter
2 eggs
½ cup sugar
2 ½ tsp. vanilla extract
3 ¼ cup flour
½ tsp. baking powder
FORTUNES, cut up and ready to insert.

## Method
Preheat oven to 425 degrees.
Beat butter, egg and sugar until smooth.
Add other ingredients and mix to form a smooth dough.
Lightly flour a board or flat surface.
Using half the dough, roll out with a rolling pin.
Roll out until less than 1/8$^{th}$ inch thick.
Use a large circle cookie cutter to cut out circles.
Place a written fortune on top of each cookie
Fold each cookie in half and then in
half again.  Pinch to close edge.
Bake in oven for about 10 minutes
or until lightly browned.
Makes about 25 cookies.

*Shh…*
*Aunt Helen wrote her*
*own fortunes for her*
*homemade fortune cookies.*

Aunt Helen was probably one of the world's worst photographers, but that didn't stop her from taking oodles of pictures wherever she went. Her photos were often blurry but her memories were always crystal clear. Pictures spilled all over the closet floor since Aunt Helen was much too busy to put them in albums.

*Aunt Helen was one of the best observers, but one of the worst photographers.*

*Aunt Helen loved to show off her zillions of photos. Never one to dress for the occasion, she giggled as she thought about the horse wearing her high heels in this double exposure.*

The photos reminded Aunt Helen of the people she met, from the men working in the fields in China to the graceful women in saris gliding through the Indian countryside. She admired the silhouette of the proud Masaii in Africa walking in the hunting ground of the king of beasts as well as the man on the beach in Bali weaving straw into a large bag.

Like the fabrics she bought, Aunt Helen wove a tapestry from the threads of peoples' lives all over the globe.

A Korogo is a type of decorative painting that is done on hand woven Kirreh cloth. Korogo paintings celebrate festivals and spirit rituals.

Aunt Helen's Korogo was painted by a member of the Korogo tribe from the Ivory Coast of West Africa. It is an original piece of African artwork that measures 9 feet long and 5 ½ feet wide.

In Africa, Aunt Helen met some pygmies who fell on the ground laughing when they saw her. It wasn't because of her blazing red hair, pale white skin or her twinkling blue eyes. It was her freckles. They called her a polka—dotted woman.

With a wave of her hand and a cheerful toodle-loo, Aunt Helen left Africa with a carved mask, a wooden sword, a huge brimmed hat to shade her freckled face and a smile. Amused and happy, Aunt Helen always said, "Although different, we all smile in the same language."

Upon arriving home, Aunt Helen often searched the closet, but it was never quietly. Not only did she jingle and jangle with beads, belts and clanking wooden shoes, she was always strutting, strumming and singing, but never in tune.

Her record player often blared with the sounds of the places she had visited. Hypnotic sounds of the didgeridoo echoed from Australia, and once someone even heard her yodel like the man she met on a hike through the Swiss Alps.

Hiking boots, Clogs,
Wooden Shoes, Straw
Flip Flops, Slippers With
Turned—Up Toes

At times, Aunt Helen put her passport away in the jewel covered locked box from Turkey and thought about the times things did not go smoothly. She sometimes stammered and stuttered and found it difficult to explain herself, but her speech disability never stopped her from greeting everyone she met across the globe.

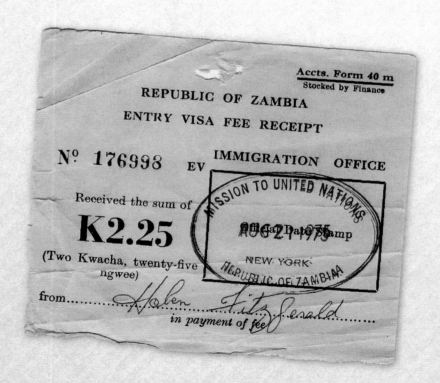

Petra, Jordan

Most of the time she planned her own trips but once when she asked a travel agent to book a trip to Bucharest, she was misunderstood. Much to her surprise, she found herself on a plane to Budapest, Hungary instead of Bucharest, Romania. Always rolling with the punches and with her favorite pocketbook on her arm, it became just another adventure to Aunt Helen and off she went.

Those who love to travel go into it with their eyes wide open. They know it won't be all, champagne, cookies and candlelight in the desert. It takes a person who can roll with the punches. And that was Aunt Helen.

**South American Cruise**

**En route from Rio de Janeiro to New York**

*Visas*

U. S. IMMIGRATION
NASSAU, BAHAMAS

SEP 30 1974

ADMITTED

POLICE NATIONALE
RENSEIGNEMENTS GÉNÉRAUX
PORT de BASSE-TERRE

Sortie **1 0 OCT. 1974**

GUADELOUPE

POLICE NATIONALE

PORT de BASSE-TERRE

Entrée **1 0 OCT. 1974**

GUADELOUPE

Most important for a world traveler, Aunt Helen had the uncanny ability to turn a negative into a positive. One of the few times she was frightened was when she visited India for the first time. Arriving in the middle of the night, she was greeted by roaming cows and screaming peacocks and no one in sight to take her to her hotel. Fortunately she was taken in for the night by an English speaking priest and his housekeeper.

Aunt Helen always said, "we all smile in the same language."

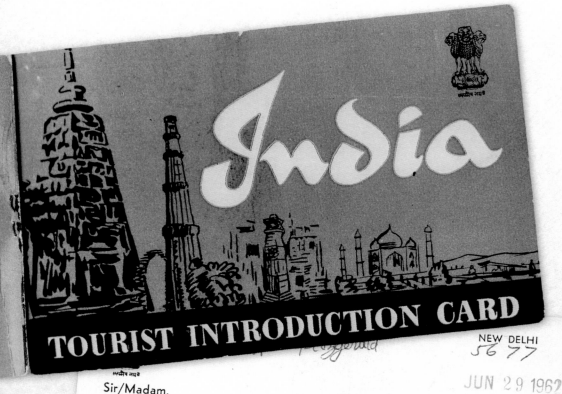

TOURIST INTRODUCTION CARD

NEW DELHI
56 77

JUN 29 1962

Sir/Madam,

On behalf of the Government of India, Tourist Division, I extend to you a cordial welcome. This card is to introduce you to the various Governmental authorities in India and to enable you to receive all possible assistance in the matter of immigration and customs clearance, booking of air and rail accommodation and for securing accommodation in Rest Houses, Dak Bungalows and Railway Retiring rooms. Our Tourist Information Officers in the various cities will be glad to be of service to you. Please feel free to call on them. We hope you will have an interesting and enjoyable sojourn in this country and that you will come back again.

*Banaras Ghats*

Secretary to the Govt. of India,
MINISTRY OF TRANSPORT & COMMUNICATIONS
(Department of Transport)

Aunt Helen made life-long friends around the world, but India was the only country she visited more than once.

DOCKYARD ROAD, MAZAGON, BOMBAY 10.

*Aunt Helen celebrating with some of the many friends that she met all over the world.*

Mgr. *Stanislaus Pereira*, Ph.L., T.D. Pastor.

ROSARY CHURCH & HIGH SCHOOL

AMOR LUCIS
19 56
ROSARY SCHOOL
MAZAGON BOMBAY

TEL. 70460

Rosary New School Building, Mazagon,
Bombay 10. India. No. 1179
ning date : 15-12-'56

ew School Building, Mazagon,
Bombay 10. India. No. 1176
ning date : 15-12-'56.

lding, Mazagon,
7

on,

78

zagon,
1179
56.

Mazagon,
118
2'56.

There was a time when Aunt Helen noticed that a boy would receive an education before a girl in India. A woman ahead of her time in interest, attitude and education, Aunt Helen donated money to begin work on a school for girls.

Creative and ingenious, when they needed cement blocks, she found a friend to supply them. When they needed more money she bought and sold raffle tickets.

Aunt Helen learned how to count money, spend money, loan money and donate money all over the world. She learned to exchange Mexican pesos for Japanese yen, Indian rupees for French francs and Italian lire for Thai baht.

| Quetzal Guatemala | Pound Ireland | Dollar Canada | Guilder Netherlands |
|---|---|---|---|
| Dollar Fiji | Lira Turkey | Deutsche Mark Germany | Dollar New Zealand |
| Rand Nambia | Peso Argentina | Dollar Hong Kong | Lira Italy |

## ARABIAN BAZAAR

SALADDIN STREET
Telephone 244 - P.O.B. 223
**JERUSALEM - JORDAN**

Oriental jewellery. Mother of ..., Rosaries, Silks, Brocades,
Embroid... ...ive Costumes, Brass Work.
...um Guide Books, and
...of Crusaders Crosses,
..., Mosaic Inlaid.

...RICES

...Destinations

And year after year back at the old house, the collection continued to grow. As she looked at each and every treasure in her closet, Aunt Helen thought about the rich life she created for herself. "A global nomad, that's what I am," she often thought.

Not wealthy with silver or gold, Aunt Helen was rich with the wealth of a traveling woman's experiences and with the memories kept alive by the treasures in her closet.

*The Many Faces of Aunt Helen*

To travel the world in her footsteps,
just step inside Aunt Helen's closet.

Happy Landing,
from all
Your friends in
the F.S.A. Unit

I think I hear Honolulu calling my name...

## Aunt Helen's Closet®
## A Museum Approach to Education

A storyteller, surrounded by exotic clothing and artifacts quiets her audience with three taps on a gong from Thailand.. She begins. "My Aunt Helen traveled to every country in the world except two and every state in the United States. She brought something home from everywhere she went and you won't believe what's in Aunt Helen's Closet."

Ellen Mnich's Aunt Helen Fitzgerald loved unique cultures, exotic places and interesting people. She spent 60 years traveling and building a collection of memories, souvenirs and artifacts that now serve as teaching tools.

Aunt Helen's Closet, an interactive, hands on museum approach to literacy and learning enables children to explore the world and its people in a motivating and meaningful manner. Weaving stories around her aunt's collection, Mnich engages audiences in lessons of cultural diversity, tolerance and the sameness of people around the world.

Aunt Helen's Closet has been featured on WTEN-TV/ABC10's Children First program and has appeared at schools, libraries, nursing homes, churches, group organizations, conferences, museums, universities and colleges.

Aunt Helen's Closet®
A Museum Approach to Education
www.aunthelenscloset.com
info@aunthelenscloset.com

Turn the page to enjoy an activity from the collection.
*Note: The following pages may be enlarged and reproduced.*

## Japanese Paper Folding

*Origami (oh-ree-gah-mee) is the Japanese art of paper folding. It has been practiced for hundreds of years. Children and adults enjoy the fun and challenge of making origami figures from paper. Most forms are made from a square piece of paper and do not require any cutting or gluing.*

### Aunt Helen's Origami House

*Directions:*

1. Use a standard size letter paper and fold the piece of paper in half.
2. Keep paper folded in half and fold down a triangle at each corner, making the lower edge parallel to the bottom of the paper.
3. Open the paper flat.
4. Push the triangle inside while folding the paper in half again.
5. Fold the right front half toward the middle, then fold the left front half toward the middle also.
6. Locate and draw a door, roof, rooms, windows, Aunt Helen and her closet.
7. Save a section for writing - describe Aunt Helen's house.

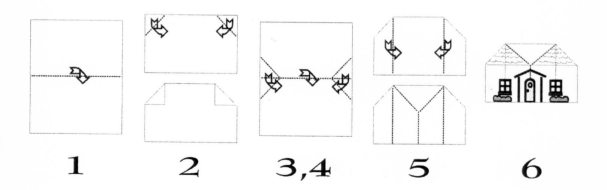

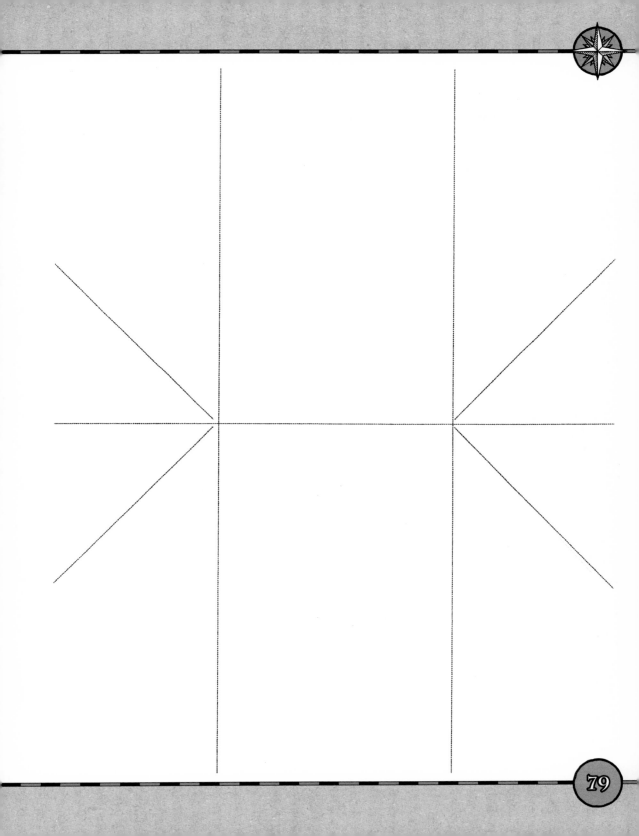

- - - - - - - - - - - - - - - - - - - - - - - - - - - - - - - - - - fold - - - - - - - - - - - - - - - - - - - - - - - - - - - -

**Festival of Nations**
**PASSPORT**

Tourist Information:

_____
_____
_____
_____

(name, age, grade, teacher)

*Aunt Helen's Closet*
A Museum Approach to Education

Directions: Copy onto colored paper of choice. Cut on the solid line, fold on the dotted lines.

*"Miss Rumphius" and "My Great Aunt Arizona"*
*are excellent books to read before a visit from Aunt Helen's Closet.*

## *"Miss Rumphius" by Babara Cooney*

*This book was given to and dedicated to Aunt Helen's Closet by the Turnpike School as a gift.*

### *Related Writing &/or Discussion Projects:*

1. Students can compare Miss Rumphius to themselves.
2. Students can compare Miss Rumphius to Aunt Arizona.
3. Point out the animals Miss Rumphius saw on her travels. Direct the students to listen for Aunt Helen's contact with animals.
4. If you were Miss Rumphius, which flower would you choose to cover the hillside?

## *Biography "My Great Aunt Arizona" by Gloria Houston*

*This book is dedicated to teachers.*

### *Related Writing &/or Discussion Projects:*

1. Discuss the characters of Aunt Helen, Miss Rumphius and Aunt Arizona and the ways in which they improved the world around them.
2. Use the words who, what, when, where and why to help the students develop questions about the three characters.
3. Ask the students if they think Aunt Arizona is someone they would like to meet? Why/not? Ask similar questions about all three characters, etc.

## Traveling Companions

### My Suitcase

1. Draw and label the items you would take on a trip. Be able to explain your choices.
2. List things to do before leaving on a trip.
3. List the first thing you'll do when you get home.

### My Luggage Tag

1. List what information should be on a luggage tag.
2. List some ways in which you could travel.
3. Describe what you would do if you lost your luggage.

### My Postcards

1. Make a list of people that you might write on a trip.
2. Design your own postcard.
   a. On one side draw a picture from a real or imagined trip.
   b. On the other side write a note to a friend about that trip.
   c. Exchange postcards with other students/classes.

To: _____

_____

_____

From: _____

To: _____

_____

_____

# My Aunt Came Back
### *Author Unknown*

*Add your own verse to this poem about Aunt Helen.*

*Have children add a verse to the poem, leaving the "sillies like you" stanza as the final verse.*

1
Well, my Aunt came back,
From Timbuktu,
And brought with her,
A wooden shoe.

5
Well, my Aunt came back,
From County Clare,
And brought with her,
A rocking chair.

2
Well, my Aunt came back,
From Old Japan,
And brought with her,
A waving fan.

6
Well, my Aunt came back,
From Old Nepal,
And brought with her,
A ping pong ball.

3
Well, my Aunt came back,
From Old Tangiers,
And brought with her,
Some pinking shears.

7
Well, my Aunt came back,
From the City Zoo,
And brought with her,
Some sillies like you.

4
Well, my Aunt came back,
From Guadalupe,
And brought with her,
A hula-hoop.

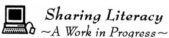 Sharing Literacy
~A Work in Progress~

Submit your verse to my e-mail address:  www.aunthelenscloset.com
Keep in touch to see the poem grow!

## A World of Difference?

**Questions:**

☺ Make a list of 3 things children all over the world would probably like.

☺ Make a list of 3 things children all over the world would probably do.

☺ Write 1 thing children all over the world could do to bring peace to the world.

☺ Write 1 thing children all over the world could do to make the world a better place in which to live.

☺ Write the first thing you would show a new student from a foreign country at school.

☺ Write the first 5 things you would teach a student from a foreign country to say.

☺ Write 2 things you would tell a person living in another country about what it is like where you live.

# How do you see the world?

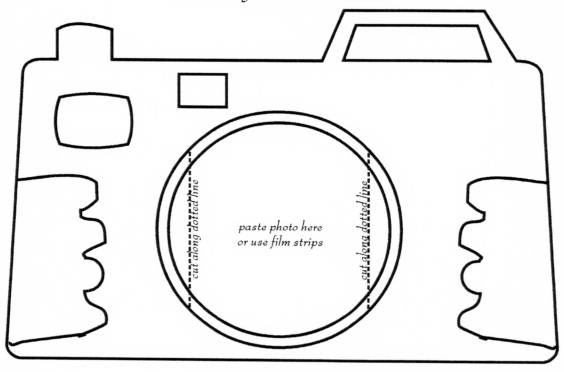

cut along dotted line

cut along dotted line

paste photo here
or use film strips

## A photograph tells a story about you.

Name _____

Subject _____ Date _____

*A photograph tells a story about you.*

*Directions: Draw or paste pictures of your experiences with Aunt Helen's Closet. For a one page project, write a brief description under each frame or cut out the film strips and use with the camera page.*

## What In the World Are They Wearing?

*How did people all over the world come to dress so differently?*
*When the first human beings were living, were they wearing any clothes?*
*Why do you prefer one outfit of clothing better than another?*

*There are many ways to study and investigate a culture. The history of fashion is one way historians, artists and scientists can find the answers.*

### Vocabulary

| | |
|---|---|
| kimono | robe worn in Japan |
| lederhosen | leather shorts worn by men and boys in Germany |
| apron | an article of clothing worn over regular clothing to protect, eg. when cooking In France and the Ukraine, an apron is worn on top of a girl's skirt as part of the outfit. |
| gele | an African turban worn on the head with all the ends tucked in |
| moccasins | American Indian foot coverings or shoes made of animal skins |
| obi | a wide sash wrapped twice around a Japanese girl's waist as part of an outfit |
| foustanella | a Greek soldiers uniform including a red cap and vest and white pleated skirt |
| kilt | a pleated, plaid skirt worn by Scottish men and boys |

| Trivia | Fact |
|---|---|
| People like to decorate themselves. | People need clothing for protection from the weather. They need less clothing where it is warm and more where it is cold. |
| They like to dress up and show off. | |
| People developed unusual clothing to scare their enemies. They wanted to scare away evil spirits. | Special clothes are worn for special occasions, for example; weddings, parades, religious celebrations, parties, holidays, etc. |
| In some parts of the world, people still believe that certain colors, patterns, and decorations will keep them from harm. | We still have rules about clothing. Schools have dress codes. The military has uniforms. Sports teams have uniforms. Restaurants and resorts sometimes require men to wear a sports jacket and women to wear dress pants or skirts. |
| A long time ago, in Europe, the color purple could only be worn by royalty. | |
| Schools show support for their team by wearing certain colors or shirts with team logos. | Formal attire is required when attending a high school prom. |
| The royalty in Hawaii, at one time, were the only ones allowed to wear the beautiful feather capes. | Throughout the world, clothes are made to be comfortable and easy to work in. |
| | In the United States, teenage girls often trade clothes including formal attire. |
| Amish people wear plain, dark clothes without buttons. The way they dress is part of their lifestyle and religious practice. | Up until 1940, fashion had always been made for adults, no one had designed clothing especially for children and teenagers. |
| Colors can mean different things to different cultures. | |

## Topics for discussion:
1. Name some people that wear uniforms. How can we determine rank or position?
2. Describe your favorite outfit.
3. Tell of a special occasion and how you would dress.
4. A long time ago, in some parts of the world, the leader could be identified by his/her hairdo, headpiece, or by an object held in their hands. Discuss people in your community that you can identify by the manner in which they dress.
5. How do you feel about 'hand me down' clothes? Describe an article of clothing that you received this way.

# Discovering Archeology

*Archeology is a way of studying the past. An artifact is anything made or used by people. An artifact tells us or gives us clues about...*

1. *where people lived*
2. *how long ago they lived*
3. *what their everyday life was like*

**Assignment:** *Be a student of archeology...*

✏ Try to understand what went on at the particular location where the artifact was found (at a dig site, classroom, closet, basement, attic, etc.)

✏ Analyze and figure out what the artifact's uses were by carefully looking at the object and asking questions...

| | |
|---|---|
| What is it made of? | Is it in tact or in pieces? |
| What could it be used for? | What is it? |
| How old is it? | Who used it? |

✏ Make a list of items, keep a log of your discoveries and analyze or examine each one using the examination chart provided.

<u>*Suggestion:*</u>  <u>Discuss the process used by archeologists at a dig site.</u>
Before objects are removed from the ground, photographs are taken to show their location at the site. As artifacts are carefully unearthed, by brushing away dirt, the pieces are collected, numbered and logged on an inventory list. The unearthed pieces and the inventory log are then brought back to a laboratory for further study and evaluation.

*Suggested books include:*
<u>*How to Dig a Hole to the Other Side of the World*</u>  *by Faith McNulty*
<u>*Mary Anning and the Sea Dragon*</u>  *by Jeannine Atkins*
<u>*Tibet Through the Red Box*</u>  *by Peter Sis*

# Artifact Examination Chart

Artifact Number:_____

Artifact Description:_____

_____

_____

_____

_____

Photograph or Drawing of Object

What is the artifact made of? (circle all that apply)

glass    wood    plastic    metal    leather    cloth    rock    paper    other

Is the artifact in tact (whole) or incomplete (only part of it)?  (circle one)

Where was the artifact found? _____

Who used the artifact? _____

What was the artifact used for? _____

_____

Archeologist Information: (name, age, grade, teacher)  Date: _____

_____

*Various Quotes from "A Traveler's Diary" - Running Press:*

☞ A journey is a person in itself; no two are alike. And all plans, safeguards, policies and coercion are fruitless. We find after years of struggle that we do not take a trip; a trip takes us.
~John Steinbeck, American Author

☞ Travel is fatal to prejudice, bigotry, and narrow-mindedness.
~Mark Twain, American Author

☞ Some of them seemed possessed of an incorrigible inner urge simple to take off and explore, to use whatever excuse was necessary to travel into country where no one else had been, to see where the rivers went, to find a pass through a mountain range that no one else had crossed.
~David Thompson, American Writer

☞ Keeping to the main road is easy, but people love to be sidetracked.
~Laotzu, Chinese Philosopher

☞ I think there is a fatality in it - I seldom go to the place I set out for.
~Laurence Sterne, English Writer

☞ The traveler was active: he went strensuously in search of people, of adventure, of experience. The tourist is passive: he expects interesting things to happen to him. He goes "sight-seeing."
~Daniel J. Boorstin, American Writer

☞ It is better to wear out one's shoes than one's sheets.
~Genoese Proverb

☞ Someone said to Socrates that a certain man had grown no better by his travels. "I should think not," he said; "he took himself along with him."
~Michel De Montaigne, French Writer

☞ Women have always yearned for faraway places. It was no accident that a woman financed the first package tour of the New World, and you can bet Isabella would have taken the trip herself, only Ferdinand wouldn't let her go.
~Roslyn Friedman, American Writer

## *More Quotes from "A Traveler's Diary" - Running Press:*

✏ Traveling and freedom are perfect partners and offer an opportunity to grow in new dimensions.
~Donna Goldfein, American Writer

✏ Traveling may be...and experience we shall always remember, or an experience which, alas, we shall never forget.
~J. Gordon, English Writer

✏ I was once asked if I'd like to meet the president of a certain country. I said, "No. But I'd love to meet some sheep herders. The sheep herders, farmers and taxi drivers are often the most fascinating people.
~James Michener, American Author

✏ "'Go West' said Horace Greely, but my slogan is 'Go Anyplace.'"
~Richard Bissell, American Writer

✏ The wise man travels to discover himself.
~James Russell Lowell, American Poet

✏ The border means more than a customs house, a passport officer, a man with a gun. Over there everything is going to be different; life is never going to be quite the same again after your passport has been stamped.
~Graham Greene, English Writer

✏ Every land has its own special rhythm,
and unless the traveler takes the time to learn
the rhythm, he or she will remain an outsider there always.
~Juliette De Baircli Levy, English Writer

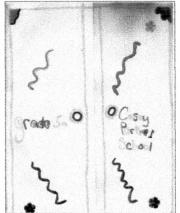

# Aunt Helen's Closet Art Project

### Create Your Own Classroom or Individual
### Aunt Helen's Closet Depicting Favorite Items from the Collection

This art project was created by the children from the Casey Park School 5th grade class and was sent to me as a thank you card telling me how much they all enjoyed a visit from Aunt Helen's Closet. They were pleased to hear that this oversized card was so wonderful that it is now part of the Collection as a resource book project. New projects for the book are always gladly accepted, so if your class creates an Aunt Helen inspired project, please send it for inclusion.

Instruct each child (or create a class list on the chalkboard) to write a list of items they remember from the collection and then place a star next to their favorite items on the list. Then have them build their closet by drawing and decorating these items which they will then glue into their own folding door closets.

## Project materials:

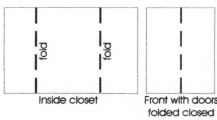

- Art/craft paper large enough to create a closet with folding doors.
- Scissors, crayons, markers, glue, glitter etc. for drawing and decorating.
- Your memory of the collection and your creativity.

## *Make an Aunt Helen ABC Book*

1. Choose a Topic
   - Animals Aunt Helen could have seen.
   - Foods Aunt Helen could have eaten.
   - Sights Aunt Helen could have seen.
   - Places Aunt Helen could have stayed.
   - Teacher or students suggestion.

2. Each child in classroom assigned a letter of the alphabet to and is asked to draw items related to the chosen topic and/or write the name under each item. This project can be adapted for any grade level.

3. Assign collating, designing a cover, binding, etc. to those students best suited for the task.

4. Trade ABC Books with other classes.

5. This is a good time to integrate with special area teachers for example: social studies, art, music etc.

6. To spark ideas, the following books from the collection may be borrowed:

   - *The Little Hebrew Alphabet Coloring Book - Jill Dublin*
   - *The Little French ABC Coloring Book - Anna Pomaska*
   - *The Little Spanish ABC Coloring Book - Anna Pomaska*
   - *Animals A-Z Around the World - Alexandra E. Fischer*
   - *The AnimAlphabet Encyclopedia Coloring Book - Keith McConnel*
   - *Ashanti to Zulu African Traditions - Margaret Musgrove*
   - *Jambo Means Hello Swahili Alphabet Book - Muriel Feelings*
   - *The Insect Alphabet Coloring Book - Julia Pinkham*

7. Donate the finished copy to the school library.

# About the Authors

Ellen Mnich has distinguished herself as a teaching artist and storyteller bringing to life the adventures of her Aunt Helen. For 15 years she has brought her museum approach to education throughout the Northeast to libraries, schools, museums and conferences. She is a member of the National Storytellers Association and Association of Teaching Artists. She was the recipient of the 2009 Girl Scout Award for Distinguished Women.

Anita DeSarbo MSEd, has worked with Mrs. Mnich to develop a portfolio of lessons designed to build language and literacy using storytelling, artifacts and literature as teaching tools. She has experience as a reading teacher, literacy and curriculum specialist and coordinator of academic programs. She is presently working at the Child Research and Study Center at the University at Albany on a project related to literacy instruction.